PIANO
DUET
PLAY·ALONG
VOLUME I

1 PIANO, 4 HANDS

PIANO FAVORITES

PLAYBACK+
Speed • Pitch • Balance • Loop

To access audio, visit:
www.halleonard.com/mylibrary

Enter Code
4723-3662-0487-2334

ISBN 978-1-4234-2124-5

Hal•Leonard®

7777 W. Bluemound Rd. P.O. Box 13819 Milwaukee, WI 53213

Visit Hal Leonard Online at
www.halleonard.com

CANDLE IN THE WIND

SECONDO

Music by ELTON JOHN
Words by BERNIE TAUPIN

Flowing, with expression

CANDLE IN THE WIND

PRIMO

Music by ELTON JOHN
Words by BERNIE TAUPIN

Flowing, with expression

R.H. 8va throughout

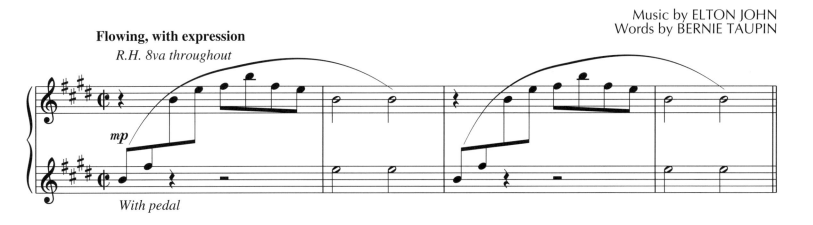

With pedal

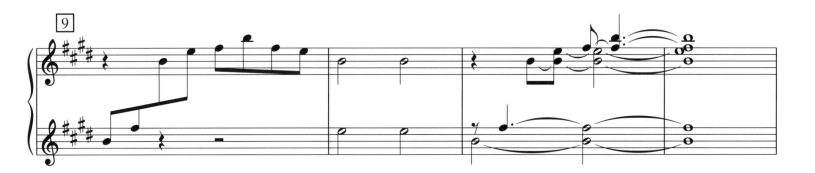

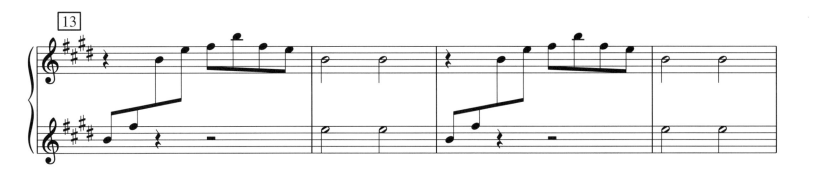

SECONDO

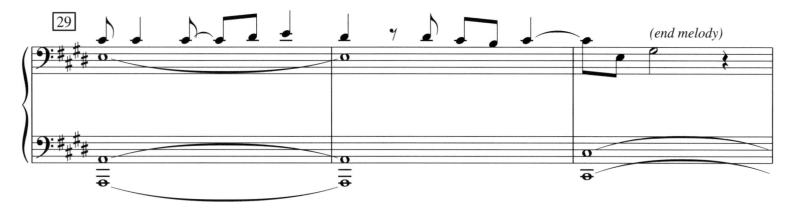

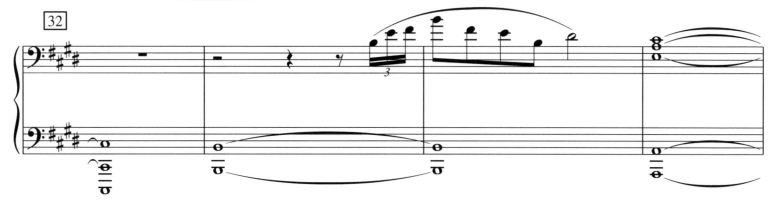

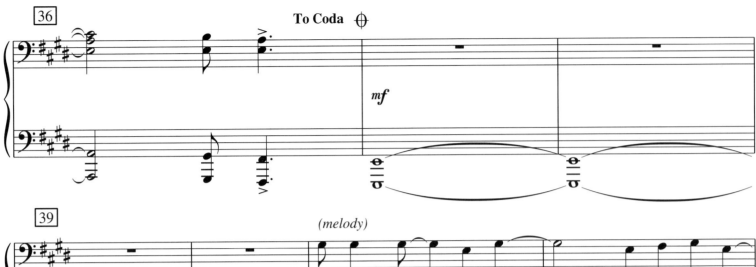

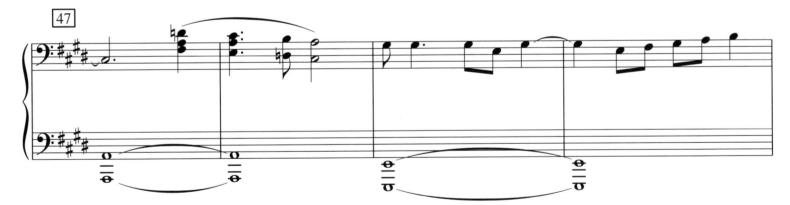

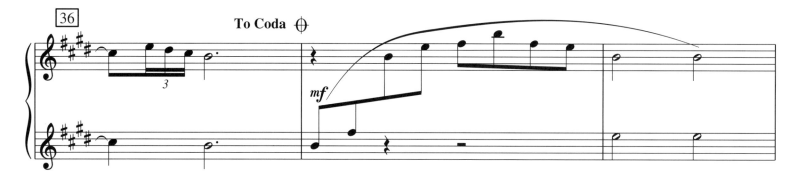

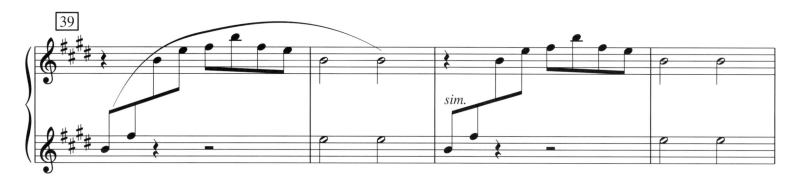

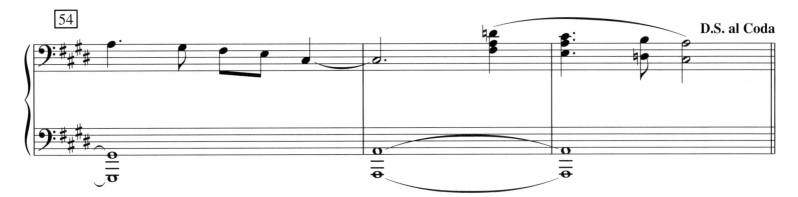

D.S. al Coda

CODA

(melody)

cresc.

f

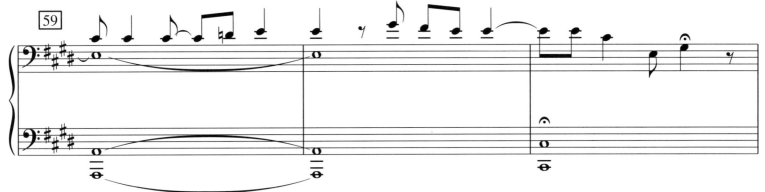

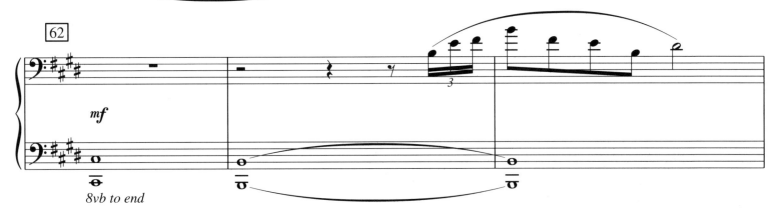

mf

8vb to end

rit.

PRIMO

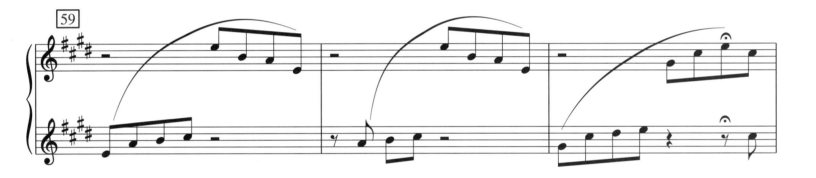

CHOPSTICKS

SECONDO

By ARTHUR DE LULLI

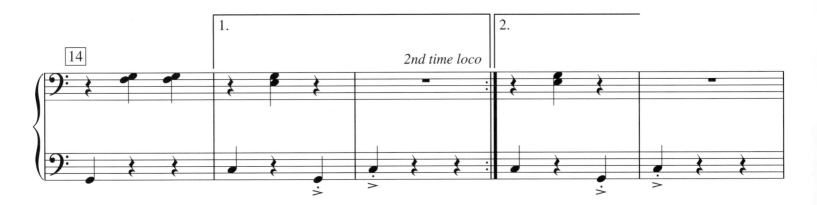

CHOPSTICKS

PRIMO

By ARTHUR DE LULLI

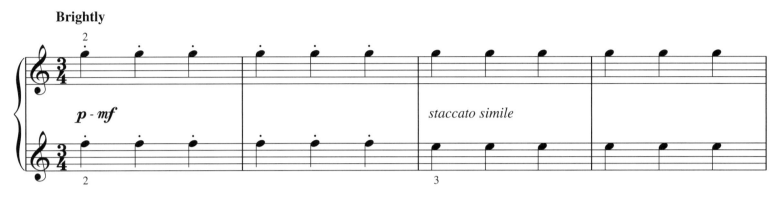

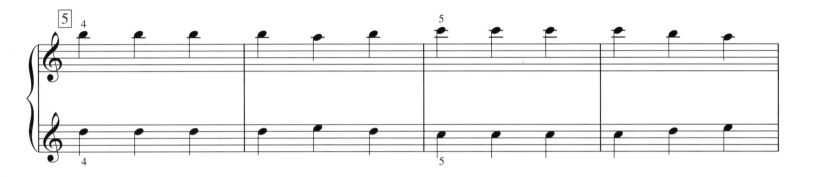

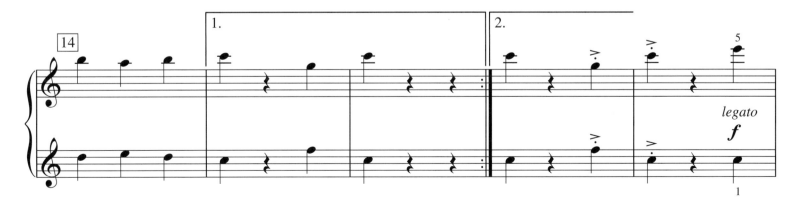

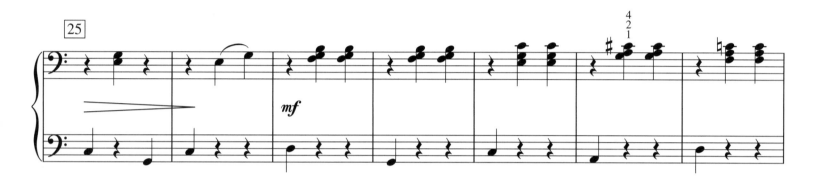

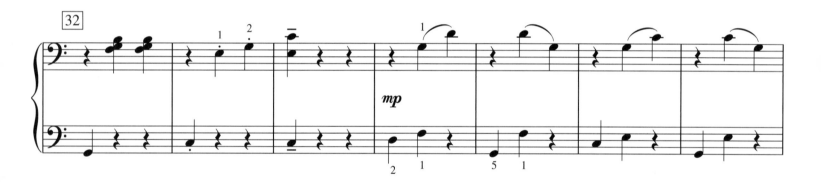

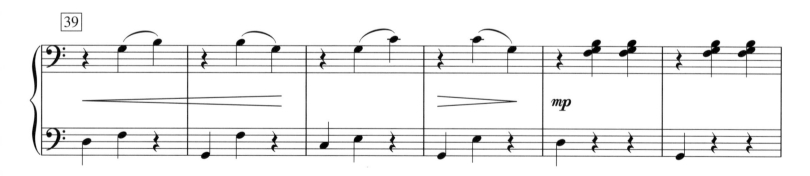

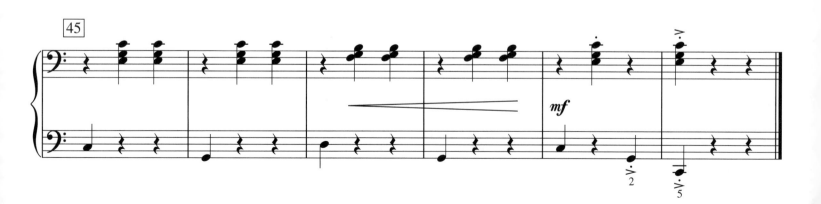

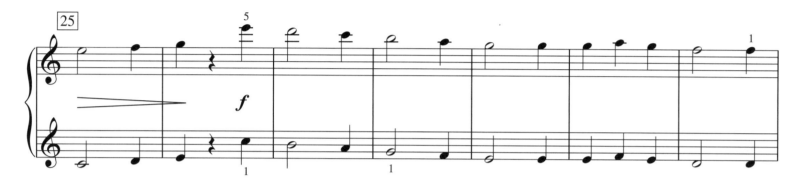

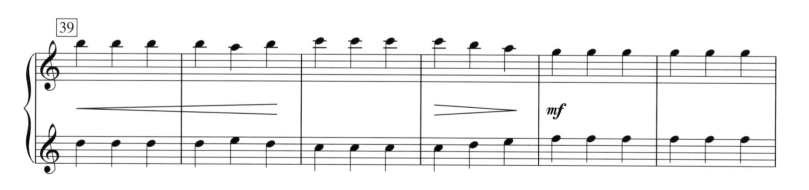

DON'T KNOW WHY

SECONDO

Words and Music by
JESSE HARRIS

DON'T KNOW WHY

PRIMO

Words and Music by
JESSE HARRIS

Moderately slow

SECONDO

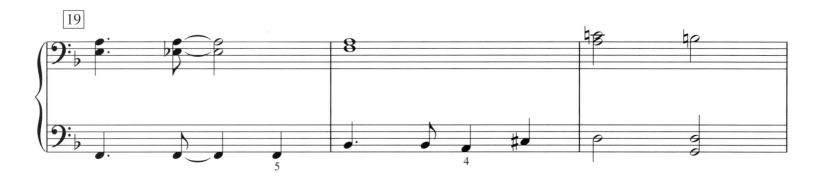

PRIMO

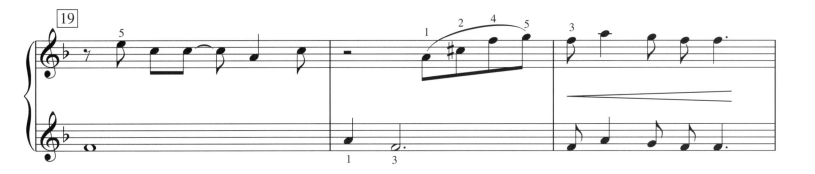

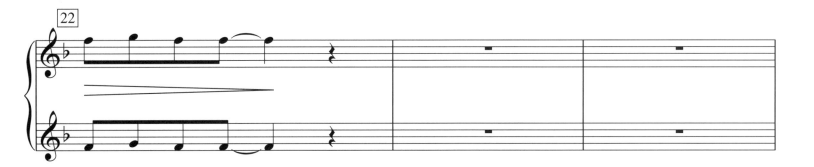

SECONDO

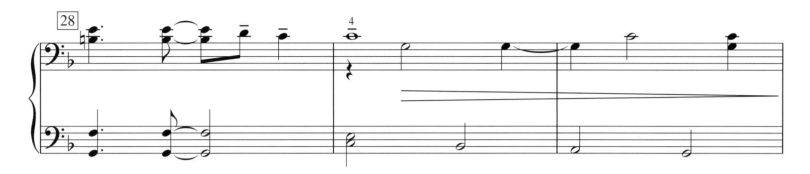

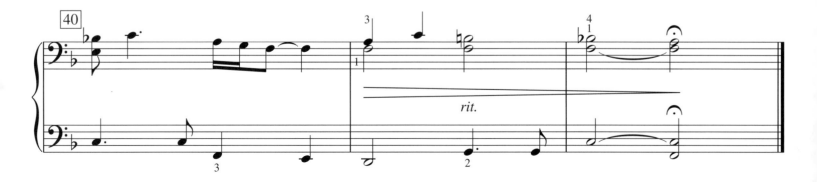

PRIMO

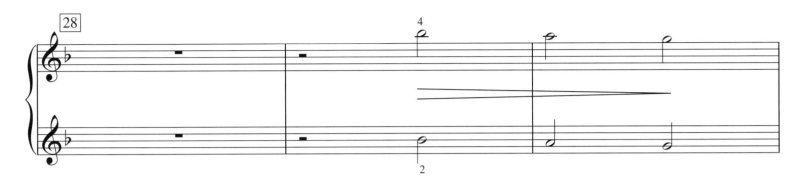

EDELWEISS
from THE SOUND OF MUSIC

SECONDO

Lyrics by OSCAR HAMMERSTEIN II
Music by RICHARD RODGERS

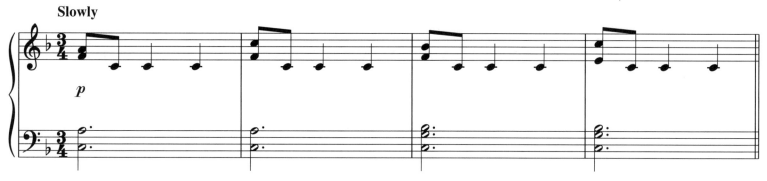

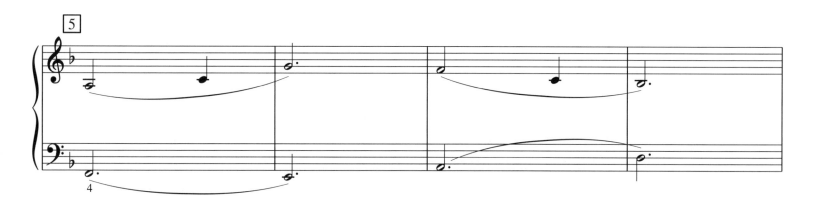

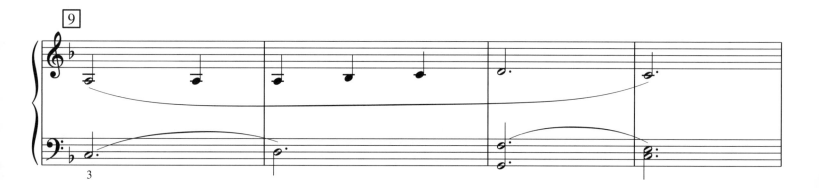

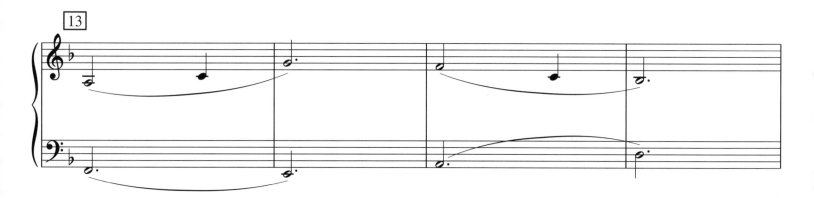

EDELWEISS
from THE SOUND OF MUSIC

PRIMO

Lyrics by OSCAR HAMMERSTEIN II
Music by RICHARD RODGERS

Slowly

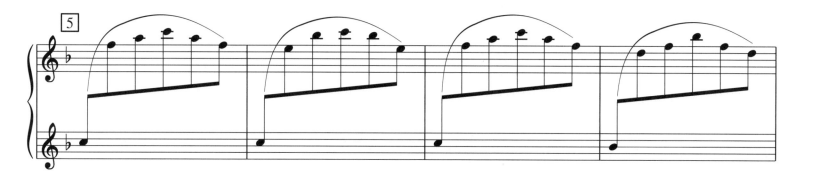

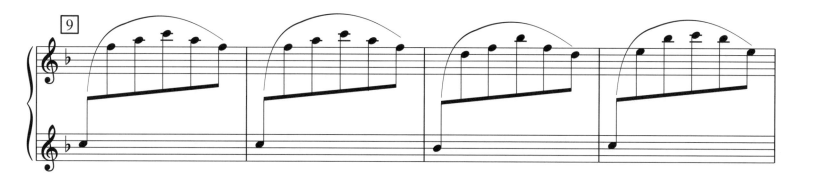

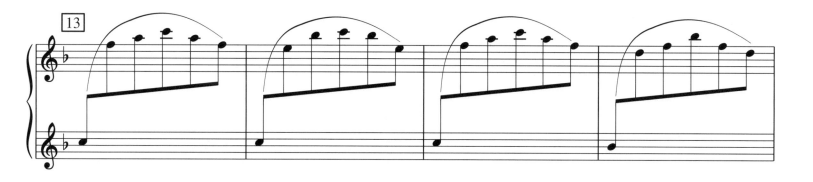

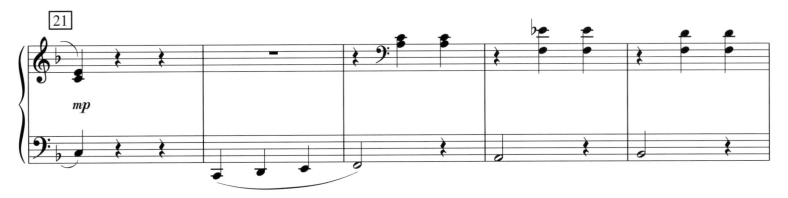

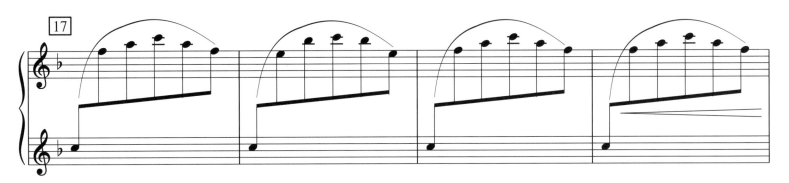

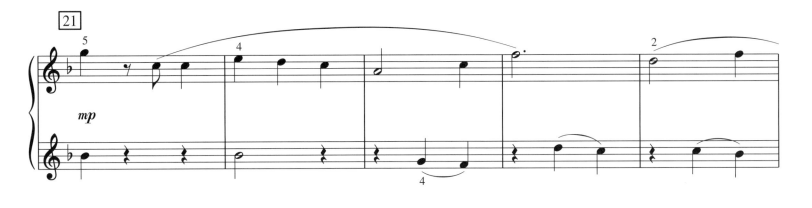

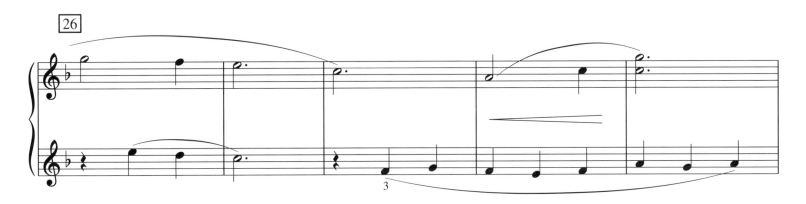

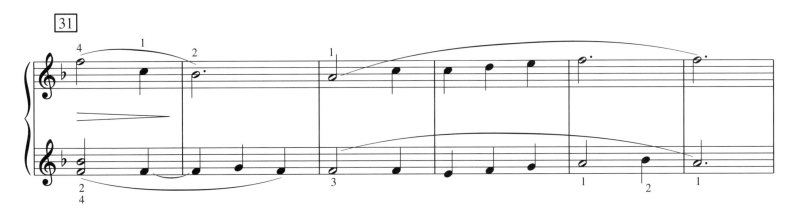

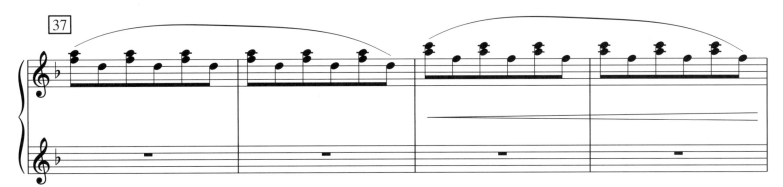

SECONDO

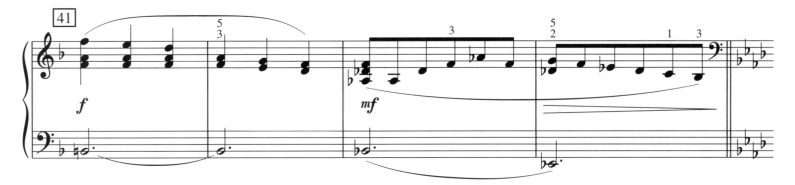

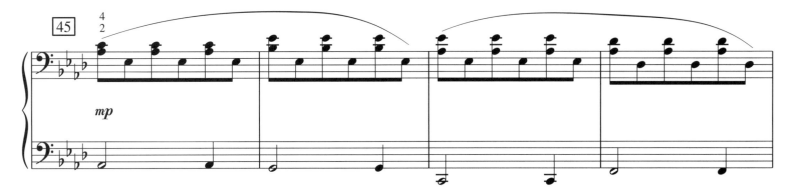

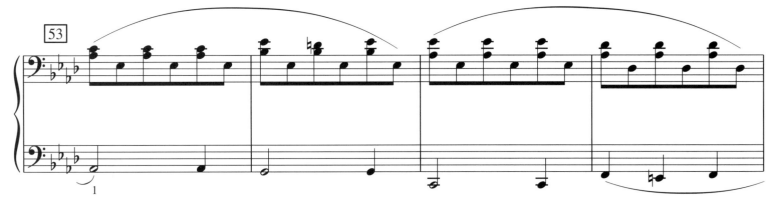

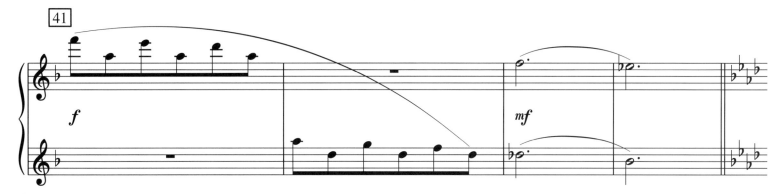

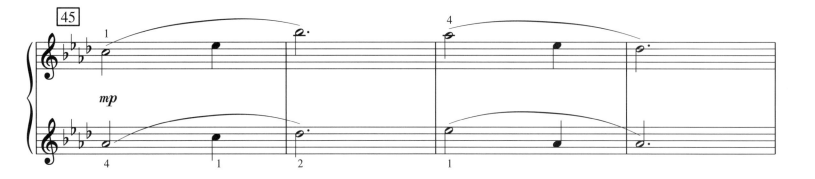

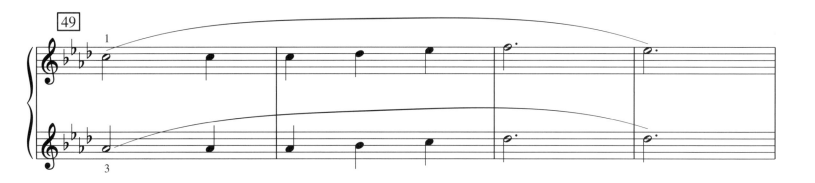

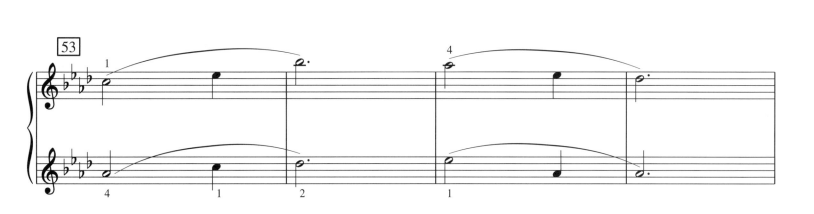

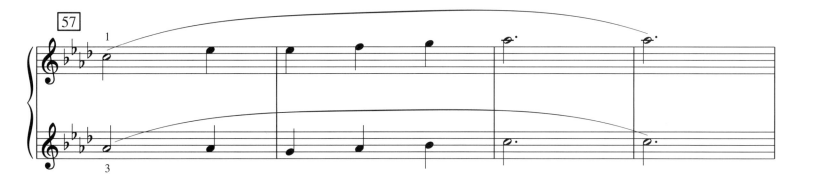

SECONDO

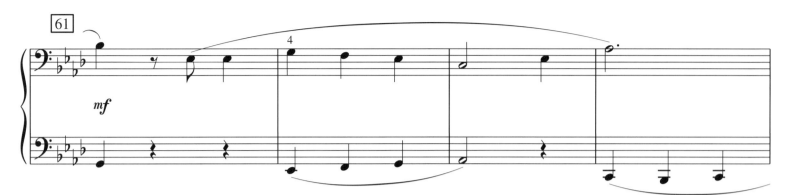

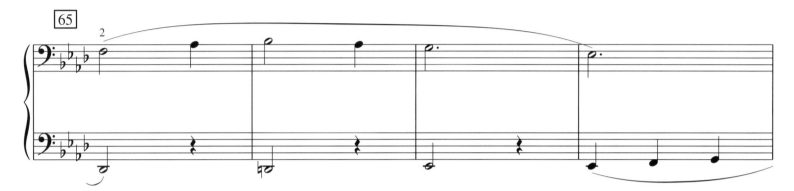

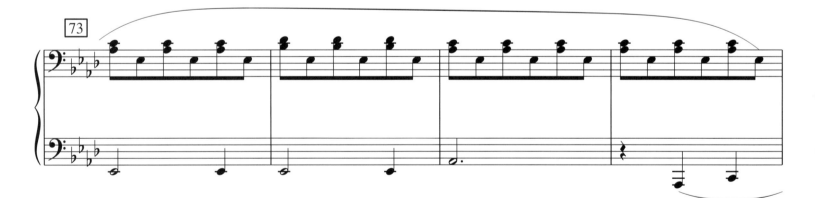

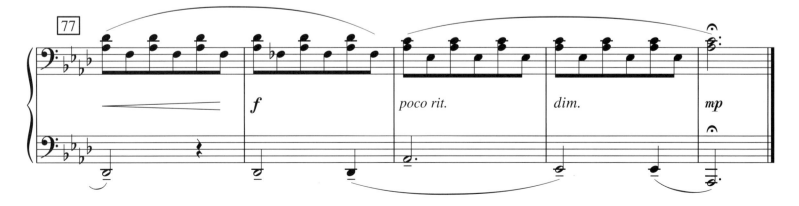

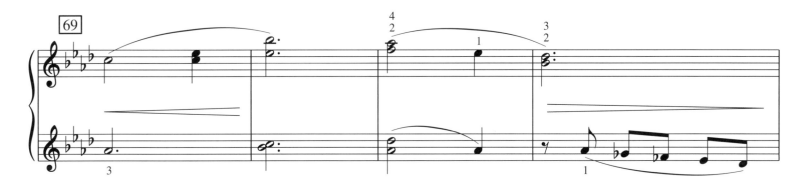

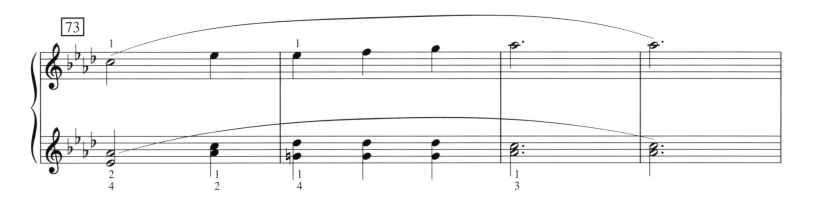

GOODBYE YELLOW BRICK ROAD

SECONDO

Words and Music by ELTON JOHN
and BERNIE TAUPIN

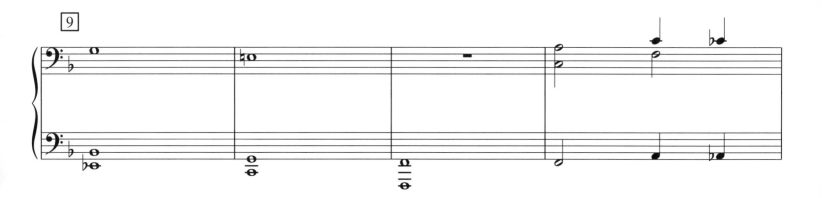

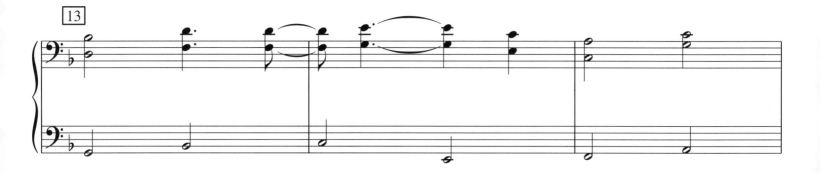

GOODBYE YELLOW BRICK ROAD

PRIMO

Words and Music by ELTON JOHN
and BERNIE TAUPIN

Slowly, in 2

SECONDO

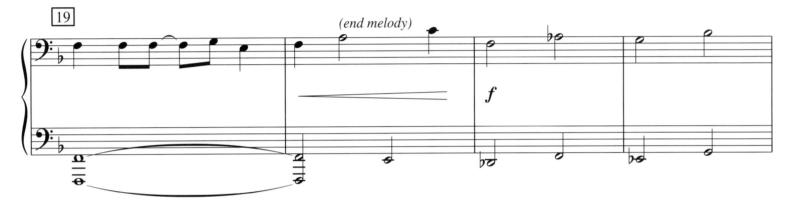

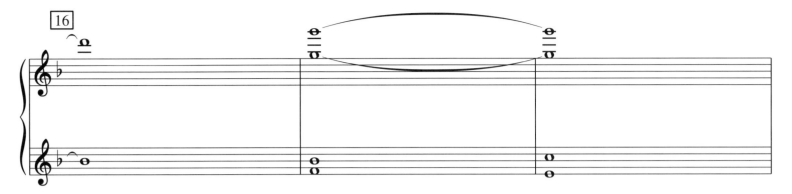

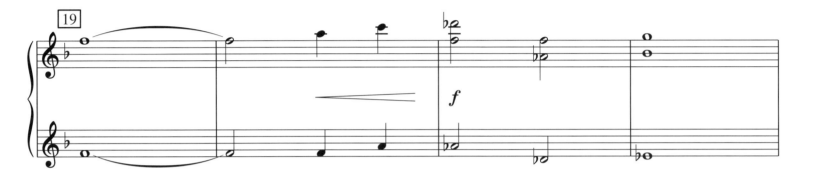

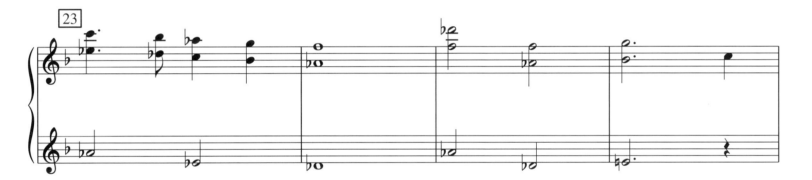

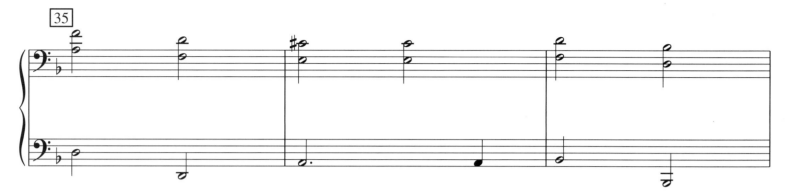

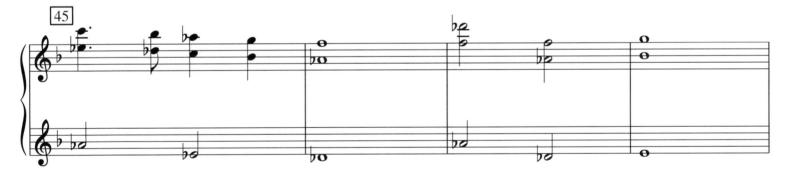

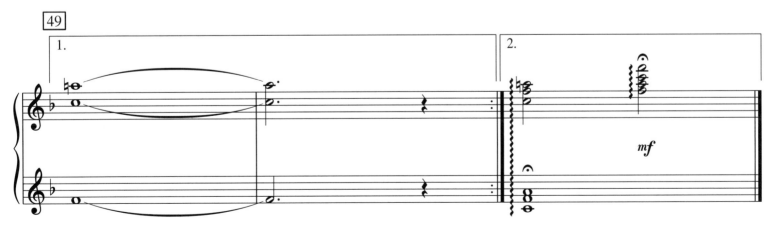

HEART AND SOUL
from the Paramount Short Subject A SONG IS BORN

SECONDO

Words by FRANK LOESSER
Music by HOAGY CARMICHAEL

HEART AND SOUL
from the Paramount Short Subject A SONG IS BORN

PRIMO

Words by FRANK LOESSER
Music by HOAGY CARMICHAEL

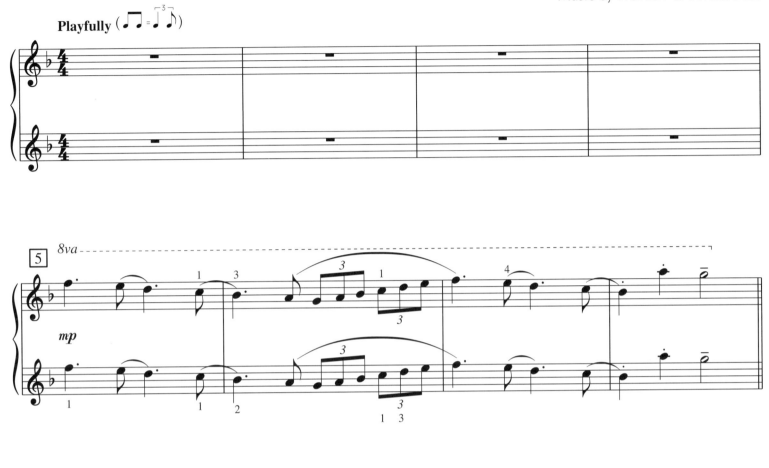

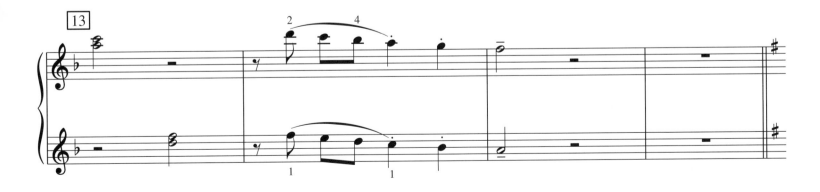

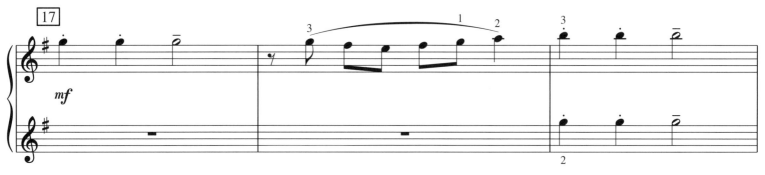

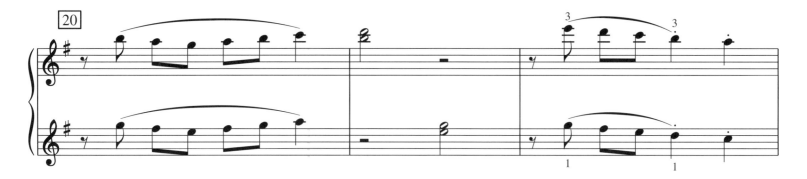

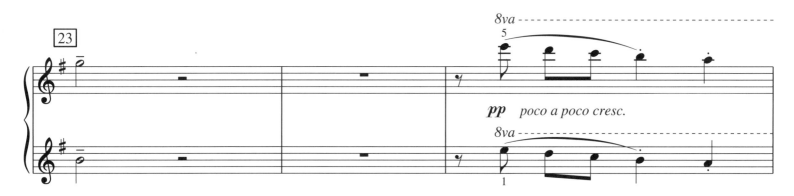

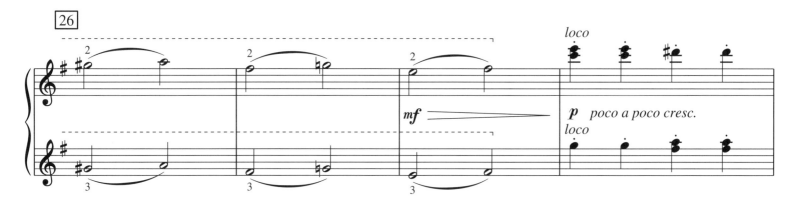

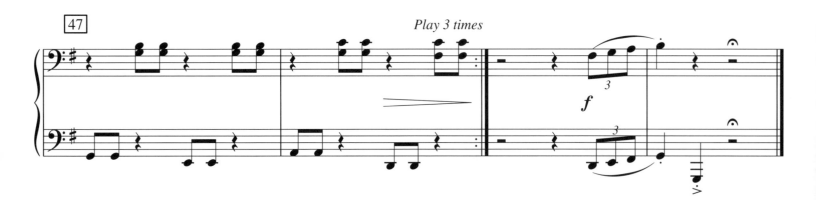

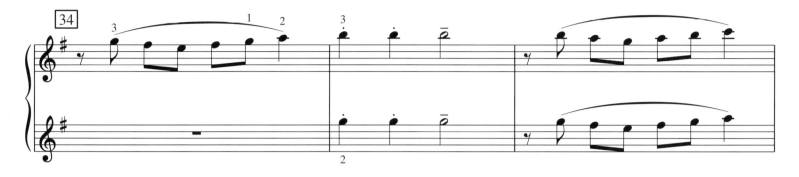

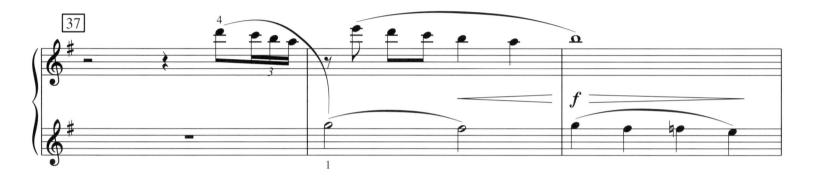

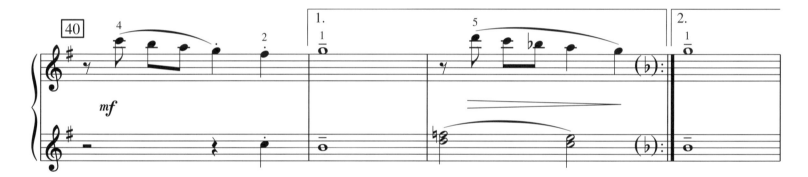

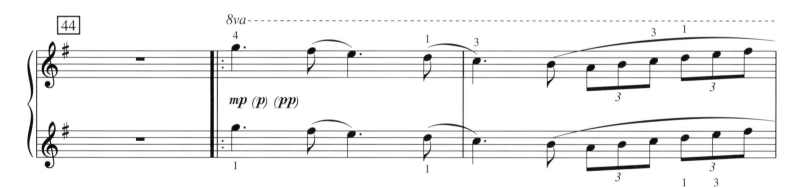

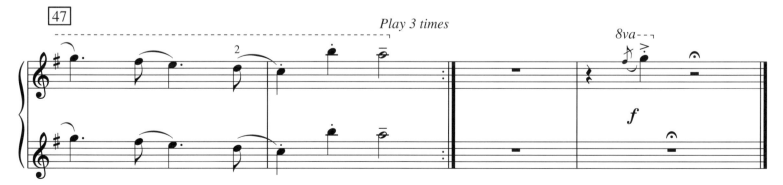

LET IT BE

SECONDO

Words and Music by JOHN LENNON
and PAUL McCARTNEY

LET IT BE

PRIMO

Words and Music by JOHN LENNON
and PAUL McCARTNEY

Slowly

SECONDO

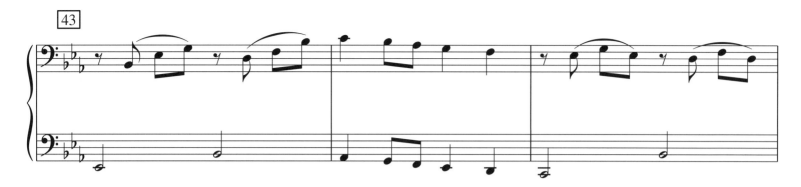

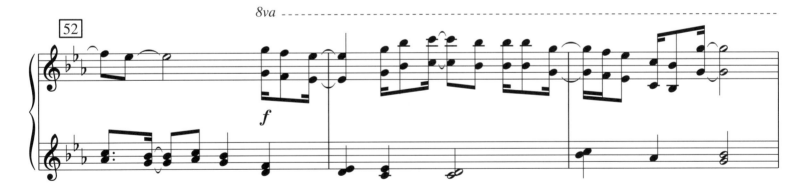

LINUS AND LUCY

SECONDO

By VINCE GUARALDI

Moderately

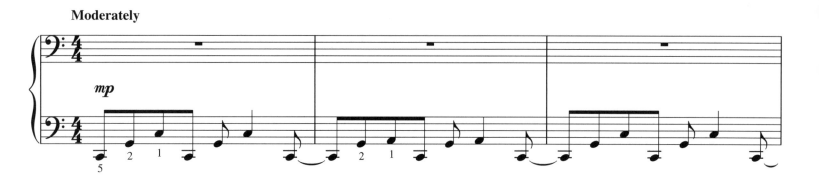

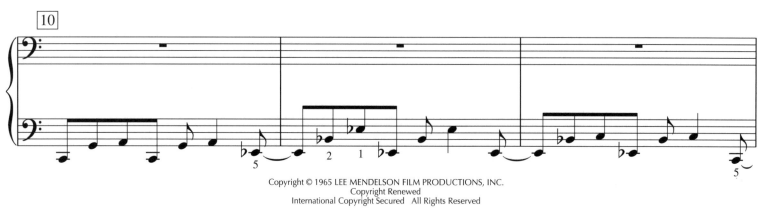

LINUS AND LUCY

PRIMO

By VINCE GUARALDI

Moderately

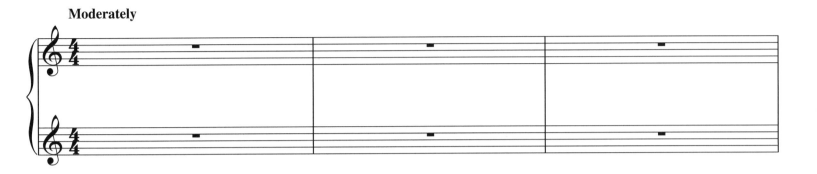

SECONDO

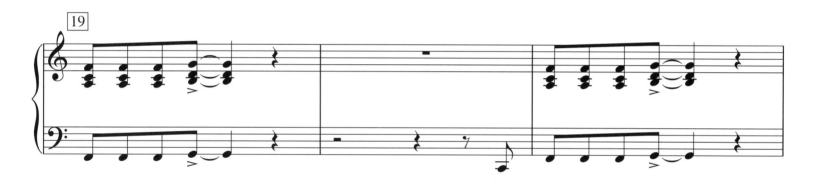

PRIMO

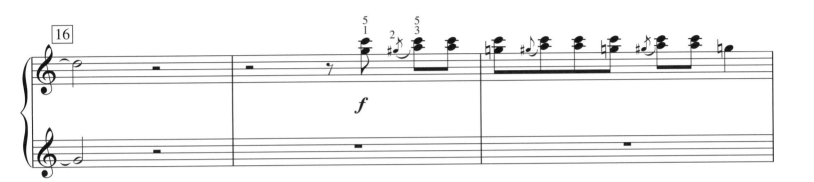

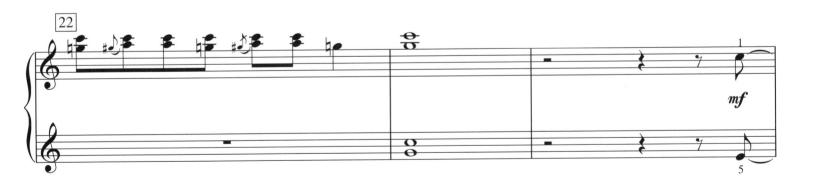

SECONDO

PRIMO

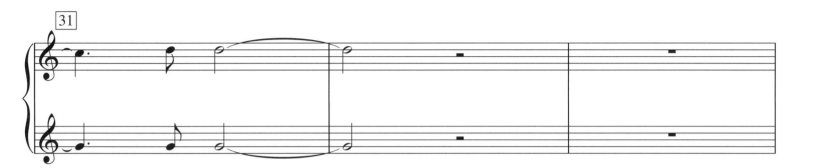

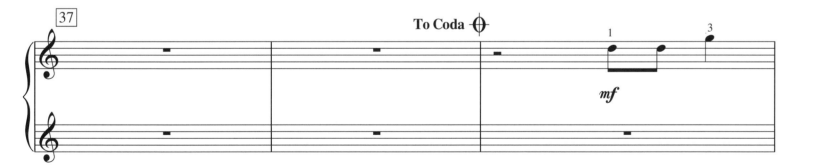

SECONDO

PRIMO

SECONDO

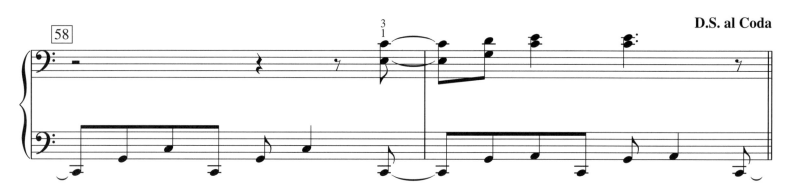

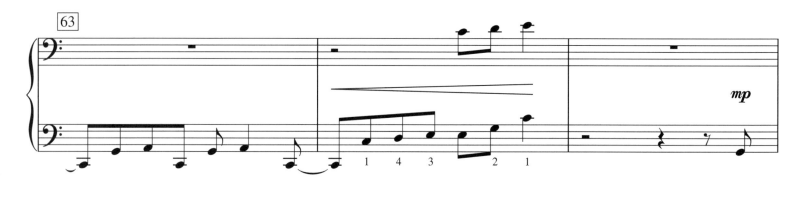

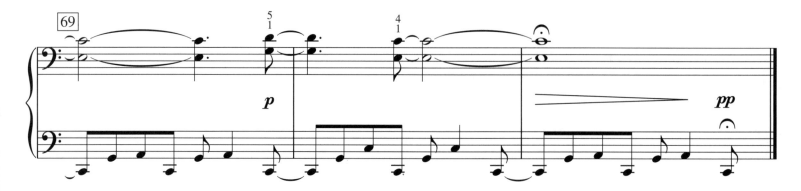

PRIMO

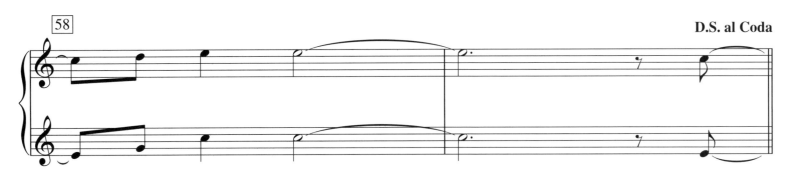

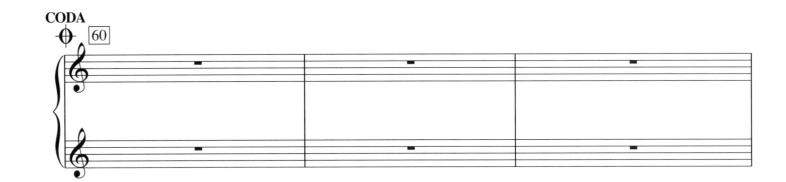

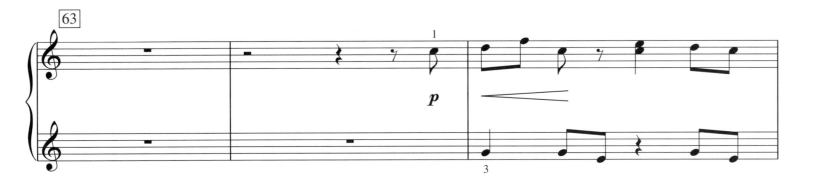

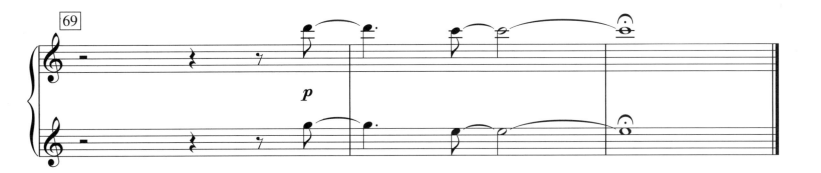

YOUR SONG

SECONDO

Words and Music by ELTON JOHN
and BERNIE TAUPIN

Slowly, flowing

mp

With pedal

YOUR SONG

PRIMO

Words and Music by ELTON JOHN
and BERNIE TAUPIN

Slowly, flowing

R.H. 8va

mp

With pedal

SECONDO

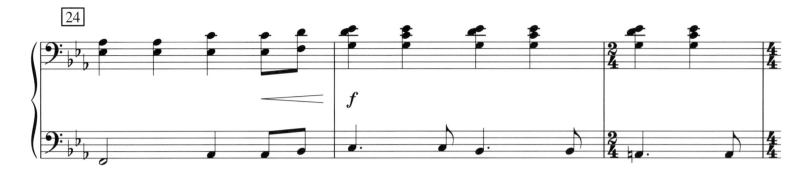

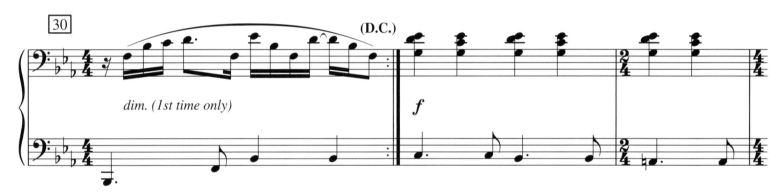

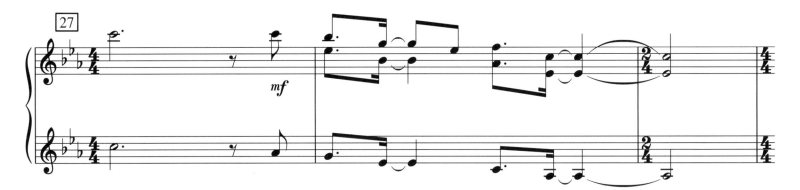

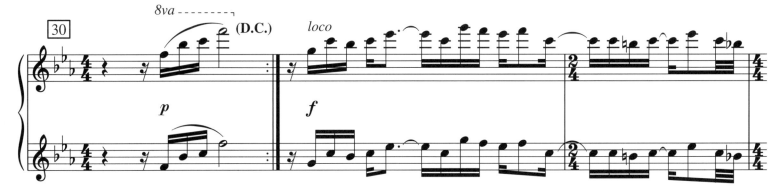

Piano for Two
A VARIETY OF PIANO DUETS FROM HAL LEONARD

ADELE FOR PIANO DUET

Eight of Adele's biggest hits arranged especially for intermediate piano duet! Featuring: Chasing Pavements • Hello • Make You Feel My Love • Rolling in the Deep • Set Fire to the Rain • Skyfall • Someone Like You • When We Were Young.

00172162.................................$14.99

CONTEMPORARY DISNEY DUETS

8 Disney piano duets to play and perform with a friend! Includes: Almost There • He's a Pirate • I See the Light • Let It Go • Married Life • That's How You Know • Touch the Sky • We Belong Together.

00128259 ....$12.99

BILLY JOEL FOR PIANO DUET

Includes 8 of the Piano Man's greatest hits. Perfect as recital encores, or just for fun! Titles: Just the Way You Are • The Longest Time • My Life • Piano Man • She's Always a Woman • Uptown Girl • and more.

00141139 ....$14.99

THE BEATLES PIANO DUETS – 2ND EDITION

Features 8 arrangements: Can't Buy Me Love • Eleanor Rigby • Hey Jude • Let It Be • Penny Lane • Something • When I'm Sixty-Four • Yesterday.

00290496.................................$14.99

EASY CLASSICAL DUETS

7 great piano duets to perform at a recital, play-for-fun, or sightread! Titles: By the Beautiful Blue Danube (Strauss) • Eine kleine Nachtmusik (Mozart) • Sleeping Beauty Waltz (Tchaikovsky) • and more.

00145767 Book/Online Audio $10.99

RHAPSODY IN BLUE FOR PIANO DUET

George Gershwin
Arranged by Brent Edstrom
This intimate adaptation delivers access to advancing pianists and provides an exciting musical collaboration and adventure!

00125150 ....$12.99

CHART HITS FOR EASY DUET

10 great early intermediate pop duets! Play with a friend or with the online audio: All of Me • Grenade • Happy • Hello • Just Give Me a Reason • Roar • Shake It Off • Stay • Stay with Me • Thinking Out Loud.

00159796 Book/Online Audio $12.99

THE SOUND OF MUSIC

9 arrangements from the movie/musical, including: Do-Re-Mi • Edelweiss • Maria • My Favorite Things • So Long, Farewell • The Sound of Music • and more.

00290389.................................$14.99

RIVER FLOWS IN YOU AND OTHER SONGS ARRANGED FOR PIANO DUET

10 great songs arranged for 1 piano, 4 hands, including the title song and: All of Me (Piano Guys) • Bella's Lullaby • Beyond • Chariots of Fire • Dawn • Forrest Gump - Main Title (Feather Theme) • Primavera • Somewhere in Time • Watermark.

00141055 ....$12.99

HAL LEONARD PIANO DUET PLAY-ALONG SERIES

This great series comes with audio that features separate tracks for the Primo and Secondo parts – perfect for practice and performance! Visit www.halleonard.com for a complete list of titles in the series!

COLDPLAY

Clocks • Paradise • The Scientist • A Sky Full of Stars • Speed of Sound • Trouble • Viva La Vida • Yellow.
00141054.................................$14.99

FROZEN

Do You Want to Build a Snowman? • Fixer Upper • For the First Time in Forever • In Summer • Let It Go • Love Is an Open Door • Reindeer(s) Are Better Than People.
00128260.................................$14.99

JAZZ STANDARDS

All the Things You Are • Bewitched • Cheek to Cheek • Don't Get Around Much Anymore • Georgia on My Mind • In the Mood • It's Only a Paper Moon • Satin Doll • The Way You Look Tonight.
00290577.................................$14.99

STAR WARS

8 intergalactic arrangements of *Star Wars* themes for late intermediate to early advanced piano duet, including: Across the Stars • Cantina Band • Duel of the Fates • The Imperial March (Darth Vader's Theme) • Princess Leia's Theme • Star Wars (Main Theme) • The Throne Room (And End Title) • Yoda's Theme.

00119405.................................$14.99

HAL•LEONARD®
www.halleonard.com